Marcos Aurélio Alves e Silva
Edelweis José Tavares

The trajectory of two math collections approved by the PNLD

Marcos Aurélio Alves e Silva
Edelweis José Tavares

The trajectory of two math collections approved by the PNLD

A journey through the triennial evaluations (1999-2014)

ScienciaScripts

Imprint
Any brand names and product names mentioned in this book are subject to trademark, brand or patent protection and are trademarks or registered trademarks of their respective holders. The use of brand names, product names, common names, trade names, product descriptions etc. even without a particular marking in this work is in no way to be construed to mean that such names may be regarded as unrestricted in respect of trademark and brand protection legislation and could thus be used by anyone.

Cover image: www.ingimage.com

This book is a translation from the original published under ISBN 978-3-330-75563-5.

Publisher:
Sciencia Scripts
is a trademark of
Dodo Books Indian Ocean Ltd. and OmniScriptum S.R.L publishing group

120 High Road, East Finchley, London, N2 9ED, United Kingdom
Str. Armeneasca 28/1, office 1, Chisinau MD-2012, Republic of Moldova, Europe
Printed at: see last page
ISBN: 978-620-8-27234-0

CONTENTS

DEDICATORY 2
ACKNOWLEDGMENTS 3
SUMMARY 5
INTRODUCTION 6
CHAPTER 1 THE BOOK AND THE PNLD IN BASIC EDUCATION 10
CHAPTER 2: MATHEMATICS IN THE TEACHING AND LEARNING PROCESS 22
CHAPTER 3 METHODOLOGY 26
CHAPTER 4. ANALYSIS AND DISCUSSIONS 30
CONSIDERATIONSFINAL 67
REFERENCES 69

DEDICATORY

I dedicate this work to two important people in my life, who will always be in my heart!

First of all to my grandfather Mr. Pedrinho *(In Memoriam)* as he liked to be called. He's not with us today, but I know how much he loved seeing everyone well. I will never forget his affection, love and the times he asked me to dedicate myself to my studies. Today I am proof of your advice and I know how important it is to me. I want to make it count in my life and one day be a little bit of what he was here on earth. Thank you, old man!

I also dedicate this work to my foundation, my inspiration and my reason for living, my mother Anabel. Whenever I look at you mainha, I know how far I can go and if I'm here today it's because even in the face of the difficulties and differences we've faced, you've always taken care of me and guided me in the right way to live. Thank you for all the scolding, stomping and ear-pulling, but also for all the love, affection, dialogue and concern. If we children knew better, we would love our mothers as much as they love us. Today I understand why they care so much. Thank you, my love!

ACKNOWLEDGMENTS

I would like to express my gratitude to everyone who contributed directly or indirectly to this work.

I thank my GOD who has always been and is with me at every moment of my life, whether good or difficult. I consider myself eternally blessed, because in the face of so many difficult circumstances, he has never forsaken me and his voice always sounds in my heart saying: "Son, don't give up, I'm with you!".

To my family for all their love and support, especially my mother Anabel, my father José Manoel and my sister Ana Kiólly, who often didn't understand why I was studying so much, but in silence respected me and gave me strength.

To the friends I have in this life and those I have met from school to university, especially those in the Best CAA Class, for all the partnership and the many moments of joy we have shared and will share. Thank you, friends! As Vinicius de Moraes once said: "I could bear, though not without pain, that all my loves had died, but I would go mad if all my friends died".

To my advisor Edelweis Tavares, for his willingness to guide me and for his support during the course of this work. To my co-supervisor Cristiane Rocha for her contributions, but above all for the many moments of conversations, advice and help during my undergraduate studies.

To Professor Ivanildo Carvalho, lecturer in CBT 2, for his contributions to this work.

To the examining board, Professors Paulo Câmara and Cristiane Rocha for their availability and contributions to improving this work.

To the teachers Ana Lùcia, Tânia Bazante, José Marcos, Elizabeth Lacerda, Viviane Lisboa and so many others who contributed to my education and were so human at many moments.

To my colleagues in the Mathematics course and especially in the Institutional Program for Teaching Initiation Scholarships (PIBID) - coordinator, supervisors and scholarship holders - a space that has contributed greatly to my education.

Finally, I would like to thank everyone who contributed in any way to this work.

SUMMARY

The aim of this study was to analyze the trajectory of two mathematics collections approved in the triennial PNLD evaluations from 1999 to 2014. The collections chosen were *Matemàtica- Imenes e Lellis* and *Matemàtica Ideias e Desafios- Iracema e Dulce* because they were present in these triennial evaluations. The analysis was based on a bibliographical survey of the critical reviews presented in the respective Textbook Guides, by means of an evaluative summary, a description of the work and an analysis of the work. The research methodology used a qualitative approach based on Bogdan and Biclen (1994) and content analysis from the perspective of Bardin (2011), both of which contributed to the analysis. Units of analysis and their respective categories were created to organize the data. Thus, it can be seen that the collections analyzed present interesting mathematical approaches for the level at which they are aimed, but with some different characteristics. We believe it is important to develop further studies and research that contribute to and support the problem studied in terms of the choice of textbook to be used in Mathematics classes, thus contributing to the students' teaching and learning process.

Keywords: PNLD, Textbooks, Teaching and Learning.

INTRODUCTION

This work arose out of a desire to look at the Mathematics Textbook Guides for Primary School II, because of the importance they play in the choice of textbooks in the country's public education system.

The National Textbook Program (PNLD) was created by Decree No. 91.542, of August 19, 1985, to replace the Textbook Program for Primary Education (PLIDEF). Its main function is to evaluate, indicate, buy and distribute textbooks to public schools. The program is linked to the National Education Development Fund (FNDE), the body responsible for its execution, and its main objective is to "subsidize the pedagogical work of teachers by distributing collections of textbooks to primary school students" (BRASIL, 2014). After evaluating the books, the Ministry of Education publishes the Textbook Guide (Guia de Livros Didâticos - GLD) with a review of the approved collections. According to Brasil (2014), the guide is sent to the schools, which choose, from the available titles, those that best meet their political and pedagogical project.

The PNLD is run in alternating three-year cycles, so each year the MEC acquires and distributes books to all students in the initial and final years of elementary school or high school. The program also caters for Special Education students.

It is worth noting that in the beginning, the evaluation criteria were more specific and mainly focused on the existence of conceptual errors, inducement to error, discriminatory practices and serious outdatedness. With each edition, the evaluation criteria were improved. "From one PNLD to the next, these criteria were improved through the systematic incorporation of multiple perspectives, readings and criticisms of the program and the evaluation parameters" (MIRANDA and LUCA, 2004, p. 127).

Students in the country's public school system will receive the following educational books:

1st and 2nd grade: linguistic literacy, mathematical literacy and complementary works (natural sciences and mathematics, humanities, languages and codes). 3rd to 5th grade: Portuguese language, mathematics, history, geography, science, regional history and regional geography. 6th to 9th grade: science, mathematics, Portuguese, history, geography and modern foreign languages (English and Spanish). In secondary school, students receive textbooks for Portuguese language, mathematics, geography, history, physics, chemistry, biology, sociology, philosophy and foreign language (English or Spanish). (MEC, 2014)

Given the importance given to the process of choosing a textbook, we can see that, before being an object of study, it becomes a mediator of knowledge, so that using it can contribute to a more critical student in the social context in which they live. Thus, we understand the relevance of this instrument in the classroom, which according to Richaudeau (1979, p. 5 apud OLIVEIRA, GUIMARÂES E BOMÉNY, 1984, p.11) "the textbook will be understood as a printed material, structured, intended or suitable for use in a learning or training process." And yet, the Textbook Guide (2014) reinforces this statement when:

> In the teaching and learning process, the textbook is an interlocutor that dialogues with the teacher and the student. In this dialogue, the textbook is the bearer of a perspective on the knowledge to be studied and on the most effective way of learning it. [...] Another function that has been performed by the textbook is to bring to the classroom didactic and pedagogical modifications proposed in official documents, as well as research results on learning mathematics. (BRASIL, 2014, p. 12)

However, the textbook is still criticized by various sectors of society for its continued production, which makes Brazil the country that produces the most textbooks in the world. On the other hand, it is important in terms of its pedagogical and economic aspects. According to Mantovani (2009) "the investments made in the PNLD have made it the largest textbook program in the world and how important it has been over the last two centuries in communicating, producing and transmitting school knowledge" (MANTOVANI, 2009, p. 20).

According to Romanatto (2004), textbooks make a number of contributions to teachers and students:

> increased ability to read (increased vocabulary, increased understanding of what is read); systematic integration of the subject (thanks to an orderly sequence of lessons); easier revision; and the development of habits of independence and autonomy. (ROMANATTO, 2004, p.6)

In short, we can see the importance of textbooks in people's lives, as they go beyond a simple school textbook, in that they live with students on a daily basis throughout their school years.

This work aims to trace the trajectory of two mathematics collections approved during the PNLD evaluations of 1999, 2002, 2005, 2008, 2011 and 2014, through their critical reviews presented in the respective Textbook Guides. The collections chosen were: *Matemàtica* - Imenes and Lellis[1] and *Matemàtica Idéias e Desafios* - Iracema and Dulce[2] , due to their presence in the last six PNLD evaluations for the final years of elementary school.

After these arguments, we have the following questions: Why have the collections analyzed remained approved in the last six evaluations and consequently present in the Textbook Guides? Are there changes with each evaluation? What changes does each collection bring with each evaluation? In order to answer these questions, it is necessary to analyze the critical reviews of the Textbook Guides, looking at the viewpoint of the evaluators.

This work is divided into four chapters. Chapter 1 gives a historical account of the textbook and the PNLD and their implications for the teaching and learning process. Chapter 2 discusses the subject of mathematics in primary education, its contributions and difficulties in the teaching-learning process, especially in the final years of this phase. Chapter 3 shows the choice of the theoretical and methodological framework, as well as its development process, and Chapter 4 reports the entire data analysis procedure, as well as its discussions.

The objectives proposed in this work are as follows:

General Objective

- To analyze the trajectory of two Mathematics collections approved in the 1999, 2002, 2005, 2008, 2011 and 2014 PNLD evaluations, through their critical reviews presented in the respective Textbook Guides.

Specific Objectives

- To observe the advances and obstacles that the collections present at each

1 Mathematics- Luiz Màrcio Pereira Imenes and Marcelo Cestari Terra Lellis. Moderna Publishing House
2 Mathematics Ideas and Challenges- Iracema Mori and Dulce Satiko Onaga. Saraiva Publishing House

evaluation from the point of view of the evaluators and how this is seen by them as positive and negative points for student learning.

- Analyze the approaches that each collection brings with it, whether they deal more predominantly with one area of knowledge or another.
- Identify whether the authors pay attention to possible criticisms in a given evaluation, or whether they remain as they are.

CHAPTER 1 THE BOOK AND THE PNLD IN BASIC EDUCATION

In view of the importance of the textbook as a resource used by teachers in the classroom and, above all, in the teaching and learning process for students, we will begin by describing a little of the historical context of the textbook as an indispensable tool in the training process. We will then go on to detail the history of the PNLD before it was given this name, as well as describing its repercussions on the educational scene.

1.1 **History of the Book and the Textbook: from the beginning to the present day**

Before books even existed, civilizations already used means of communication through cave paintings, due to the rare contact with paper. According to Schubring (2003),

> The limitations imposed on the dissemination of books before the invention of paper lay in the fact that writing materials were rare and expensive, such as parchment in Europe, or difficult to handle and preserve, such as clay tablets for cuneiform texts in Mesopotamia, papyrus in Egypt, dried palm leaves in India, etc. (SCHUBRING, 2003, p. 19).

Schubring (2003) also reports the existence of institutionalized teaching around 3,000 to 2,500 BC in Mesopotamia. *The* writing of *The Elements*, attributed to Euclid, in Hellenistic Greece, around 300 B.C. And also the discovery of two important documents in mathematical arithmetic: the Rhind Papyrus, around 1,600 B.C. and the Moscow Papyrus, around 1,800 B.C.

Other civilizations pointed to printed scripts in the 8th century. Countries such as China, Japan and Korea used terracotta or metal writing, as well as xylography, a printing technique with engraving on wood and reproduction by rubbing, like a kind of stamp.

From Modernity onwards, with the creation of the press and the circulation of newspapers, books and magazines, a new type of "reader" emerged, one who moved from the position of listener-receiver to that of assiduous and autonomous reader.

Today, we see the book in increasingly sophisticated forms, including greater portability, due to the possibility of interaction and storage on physical units, such as *tablets, pen-drives and smartphones*; and, finally, the use of the internet, which enables storage in virtual environments and access to texts anywhere on the planet.

Thus, the textbook only emerged as an instrument of instruction in the 16th century B.C. "Wisdom was intrinsic to those who almost always visited libraries and were willing to value books" (FRANSCISCO, 2005, p.18). It was the creator of Didactics Magna, Comenius, who first emphasized that certain characteristics of books would make them more suitable for transmitting knowledge.

In Brazil, the book appeared in 1808, with the arrival of the Portuguese court, bringing with it the first printing press. At the time, political dominance was exercised by the state and the church, so only articles that did not offend institutions and customs were allowed to be published. It wasn't until 1821, when the ban was lifted, that other newspapers, pamphlets and magazines appeared. Over the years, various laws and decrees concerning textbooks came into force. Gomes (2014) gives an account of moments in Brazil when textbooks were used.

Chart 1- The history of textbooks in Brazil.

Year/Historical period	Description
1930-1945 (New State)	-More consistent public policies on teaching materials, to the detriment of the first activities developed by the Estado Novo with regard to educational resources; -Officialization and regulation of the first policy to legislate and control the production of textbooks. And the establishment of the National Textbook Commission (CNLD). All through Decree n. 1.006, of 30/12/1938.
1964-1984 (Military Regime)	-New educational agreements; -Agreements between the Ministry of Education (MEC) and the United States Agency for International Development (USAID) to provide technical training through textbooks; -Severe control over the educational system and teaching materials in order to meet the demands of the new school context that was about to emerge.
1985	-After the end of the military period, a new program was created, responsible for the purchase and distribution of textbooks, the PNLD (National Textbook Program), through Decree No. 91.542. This program remains in place to this day.
1990	-More systematic discussion by the Ministry of Education (MEC) on the

	quality of textbooks; -New pedagogical projects disseminated through the textbook guides and the National Curriculum Parameters (PCN).
1996	-The process of pedagogical evaluation of the books registered for the 1997 PNLD begins.
2010	-Decree 7084, of January 27, 2010. Regulates the participation of schools and procedures for choosing textbooks in the PNLD.

Source: Gomes (2014)

Thus, it is possible to see that the trajectory involving the textbook has been of paramount importance for us today to have new conceptions regarding the approach to content and the teaching-learning methodology employed by the teacher. As a result, each year the process of choosing textbooks is carried out in a careful way so that they follow the specificities of each reality.

1.2 **The textbook as a tool in the teaching-learning process**

The school, as a place where scientific knowledge is recognized, uses the textbook in the classroom as one of the tools for validating this knowledge. The textbook has become an object that for a long time has been difficult to conceptualize, given the variables that permeate its existence. Formally, according to the Portuguese language dictionary Aurélio, *didâtico* means "relating to teaching, or proper to it; proper to instruct". From an academic perspective, Lajolo (1996) states that,

> (...) a textbook, then, is a book that will be used in classes and courses, which has probably been written, edited, sold and bought with this systematic school use in mind. (...) Thus, to be considered *didactic*, a book needs to be used systematically in the teaching and learning of a particular object of human knowledge, usually already consolidated as a school subject. In addition, the textbook is also characterized by being able to be used in the specific situation of the school, i.e. collective learning and guided by a teacher (LAJOLO, 1996, p. 1).

The National Curriculum Parameters - PCN's already mentioned the importance of using textbooks in class, but they cannot be the only tool to be used,

> the textbook is a material that has a strong influence on Brazilian teaching practice. Teachers need to pay attention to its quality, coherence and any restrictions it may have in relation to the proposed educational objectives. In addition, it is important to consider that the textbook should not be the only material to be used, as it is the variety of sources of information that will help the student to have a broad view of knowledge

(BRASIL, 1998, p. 67).

The Pernambuco State Common Curriculum Base (BBC), on the other hand, pays attention to the pedagogical function and cultural role of the textbook. In this respect, the textbook is of great value to the teaching and learning process, but it needs to be an aid and not the teacher's sole and exclusive tool. "Teachers must be vigilant so that their pedagogical autonomy is not compromised by allowing the textbook to play a dominant role in the teaching and learning process and not that of an auxiliary resource in this process" (PERNAMBUCO, 2008).

The textbook plays a very essential role in students' lives, because as well as providing support for the construction of knowledge in the subjects, it provides knowledge that touches on social experience. However, for this to happen, curricula need to be adapted to reality and correspond to the new moment proposed by contemporary education. According to Sposito (2006),

> [...] it must be compatible with its pedagogical project, with the proposed curriculum, with the existing structure and resources, and with the school's working conditions. Finally, the book must make it possible to articulate with other areas of knowledge (SPOSITO, 2006, p. 25).

In addition, the textbook guide of the National Textbook Plan (PNLD) of 2008 already discussed the role of the textbook in the context of the student,

> it should be noted, however, that the possible functions that a textbook can perform do not become reality if the context in which it is used is not taken into account. In other words, the functions mentioned above are historically and socially situated and therefore subject to limitations and contradictions. For this reason, both when choosing and using a textbook, the teacher has the indispensable role of observing the suitability of this didactic instrument for their teaching practice and their pupil. (BRASIL, 2007, p.12)

The guide also states that the textbook should not be the only resource to be used in the classroom, but should be complemented by other resources. However, when we look at the reality of the teacher, we see that the textbook will often be the only object used to teach the class. This is due to a lack of investment in new teaching resources, the socio-economic vulnerability of the teacher or even the precariousness of the teacher's training, who is at the mercy of using what is available to them and carrying out their lessons with a single object. Barreto and Monteiro (2012) point out one of these truths when they report that "Many lessons to be given per day, sometimes in different grades, end up forcing the teacher to follow the activities or tasks proposed in the textbook with the students in the classroom".

Similarly, most of the time the student's only contact with an object of knowledge at school is limited to the textbook, and this happens from the first years of basic schooling until the end. Hence the need for greater dialogue between teacher and student and also with the reality outside school.

1.3 **History of the National Textbook Program (PNLD)**

The history of the National Textbook Program begins long before the program was given that name. According to the Ministry of Education - MEC, the program is the oldest of the programs aimed at distributing textbooks to students in the Brazilian public school system. Let's look at these moments according to Brasil (2014).

1929 - The State creates a specific body to legislate on textbook policies, the National Book Institute (INL), helping to give greater legitimacy to the national textbook and, consequently, helping to increase its production.

1938 - Through Decree-Law No. 1.006, of 30/12/38, the State establishes the National Textbook Commission (CNLD), establishing its first policy of legislation and control over the production and circulation of textbooks in the country.

1945 - By Decree-Law No. 8.460, of 26/12/45, the State consolidates legislation on the conditions for the production, import and use of textbooks, restricting the teacher's choice of the book to be used by the students, as defined in Article 5.

1966 - An agreement between the Ministry of Education (MEC) and the United States Agency for International Development (USAID) led to the creation of the Technical and Textbook Commission (Colted), with the aim of coordinating actions relating to the production, publishing and distribution of textbooks. The agreement guaranteed MEC sufficient resources to distribute 51 million books free of charge over a three-year period. By guaranteeing government funding from public funds, the program had the character of continuity.

1970 - Decree No. 35 of March 11, **1970** from the Ministry of Education implements the book publishing system with national publishers, with funds from the National Book Institute (INL).

1971 - The National Book Institute (INL) starts to develop the Textbook Program for Primary Education (Plidef), taking over the administrative and financial resource management tasks that had been Colted's responsibility until then. The contribution of the federal units became necessary with the end of the MEC/USAid agreement, and became effective with the implementation of the system of financial contributions from the federal units to the Textbook Fund.

1976 - By Decree No. 77.107, of February 4, 1976, the government takes over the purchase of a good portion of the books and distributes them to schools and federal units. With the extinction of INL, the National School Material Foundation (Fename) became responsible for implementing the textbook program. The funds come from the National Education Development Fund (FNDE) and from contributions from the minimum counterparts established for participation by the federal units. The vast majority of municipal schools are excluded from the program due to insufficient resources to serve all elementary school students in the public school system.

1983 - In place of Fename, the Student Assistance Foundation (FAE) is created, incorporating Plidef. At the time, the working group in charge of examining problems relating to textbooks proposed that teachers should be involved in choosing the books and that the program should be expanded to include the other elementary school grades.

1985 - Decree No. 91.542 of 19/8/85 gave way to the National Textbook Program (PNLD).

1992 - The distribution of books is jeopardized by budget limitations and *there is* a setback in the scope of distribution, restricting it to the 4th grade of elementary school.

a

1993 - In July 1993, FNDE Resolution No. 6 earmarked funds for the purchase of textbooks for public school students, thus establishing a regular flow of funds for the purchase and distribution of textbooks.

1995 - Gradually, the universal distribution of textbooks in primary education is resumed. In 1995, the subjects of mathematics and Portuguese were covered. In 1996, science and, in 1997, geography and history.

1996 - The process of pedagogical evaluation of the books registered for the 1997 PNLD begins. This procedure was improved and is still being applied today. Books with conceptual errors, inducements to error, outdatedness, prejudice or discrimination of any kind are excluded from the Textbook Guide.

1997 - In February, the Student Assistance Foundation (FAE) was abolished and responsibility for implementing the PNLD policy was transferred to the National Education Development Fund (FNDE). The program was expanded and the Ministry of Education began to purchase, on an ongoing basis, textbooks on literacy, Portuguese, mathematics, science, social studies, history and geography for all students in grades 1 to 8 of public primary education.

2000 - The PNLD introduced the distribution of Portuguese language dictionaries for use by students in grades 1 to 4 in 2001 and, for the first time in the history of the program, textbooks were delivered the year before the school year in which they were to be used. The books for 2001 were delivered by December 31, 2000.

2001 - The PNLD gradually extends the provision of Braille textbooks to visually impaired students in regular public school classrooms.

2002 - With the aim of achieving the goal in 2004 of all students enrolled in elementary school having a Portuguese language dictionary for use throughout their school life, the PNLD continues to distribute dictionaries to students entering grade F and to students in grades 5ª and 6ª .

2003 - The PNLD distributes Portuguese language dictionaries to those entering grade F and to students in grades 7 and 8, achieving the goal of providing all elementary school students with educational material that will accompany them continuously in all their school activities. The Geographical Atlas is also distributed to schools that have both EJA and regular 5th to 8th grade classes.

2004 - Textbooks for all curricular components are distributed to students in grades F to 4; dictionaries to students in grades F and repeaters in grade 8 and the last replacement and complementation of the 2002 PNLD to students in grades 5 to 8. Around 38.9 million dictionaries are also given to students for their personal use. The dictionary is the property of the student, who can share the research source with the whole family.

2005 - Textbooks are distributed for all curricular components in grades F, 2 to 4, replacement and supplementation, and to all students in grades 5 to 8.

From 2005 onwards, the system for distributing dictionaries was reformulated in order to prioritize the use of the material in the classroom. Thus, instead of delivering a book to each student, the FNDE provides dictionary collections to all public schools from grades 1ª to 4ª . The books are also adapted to the student's level of education, as follows:

. Type 1 dictionaries - with 1,000 to 3,000 entries, suitable for introducing children to this type of work.

. Type 2 dictionaries - with 3,500 to 10,000 entries, suitable for students who are in the process of consolidating their writing skills.

. Type 3 dictionaries - with 19,000 to 35,000 entries, aimed at students who are beginning to master writing.

Classes in grades F and 2 receive type 1 and type 2 dictionaries, while those in grades 3 and 4 receive types 2 and 3. In public schools that adopt nine-year primary education, the first group is made up of students in grades 1 to 3 and the second group is made up of those in grades 4 and 5.

2006 - Distribution of textbooks for all curricular components in the 1st grade; the second complement of the PNLD/2004 to students in the 2nd to 8th grades and the first replacement and complement of the PNLD 2005 to students in the 5th to 8th grades. Dictionaries were purchased for school libraries. Distribution of a trilingual illustrated encyclopedic dictionary - Brazilian Sign Language/Portuguese Language/English Language - to students who are deaf and use the Brazilian Sign Language (Libras).

2007 - The FNDE buys 110.2 million books for replacement and supplementary enrollment for grades 2 to 4 (3rd to 5th year) and the complete curriculum for students in grades 1 and 5 to 8 (1st and 2nd and 6th to 9th year) to benefit 31.1 million students in 139,800 public schools in the 2008 school year. It is also buying trilingual dictionaries in Portuguese, English and Libras to supply deaf students in primary and secondary schools. Students with deafblindness in grades 1 to 4 also receive a booklet and a Portuguese language book in pounds and on CD-ROM.

In addition, 18.2 million books were purchased for 7.1 million students in 15.2 thousand public secondary schools. In line with the progressive goal of universalization of textbooks for secondary education, the textbook package was expanded with the purchase of history and chemistry textbooks. The range was completed in 2008 with the purchase of physics and geography textbooks.

2008 - Distribution of textbooks for all curricular components, literacy, Portuguese language, mathematics, history, geography and science for grades 1ª , 5ª to 8ª and replacement and supplementation for students in grades 2 to 4.

1.4 **National Textbook Program (PNLD): Evaluation process and criticism**

The PNLD is an extremely important program in terms of organizing the structure of textbooks in the country and has brought about changes in their acquisition, such as:

> Indication of the textbook by the teachers; Reuse of the textbook, implying the abolition of the disposable textbook and the improvement of the technical specifications for its production, aiming at greater durability and making it possible to set up textbook banks; ªExténding the offer to 1st and 2nd grade students in public and community schools; Ending the financial participation of the states, handing over control of the decision-making process to the FAE (Student Assistance Foundation) and guaranteeing the criterion of the teachers' choice of textbook. (BRAZIL, 2012).

In 1996, the process of evaluating textbooks began, initially for grades 1 to 4, culminating in the preparation and publication of the first Textbook Guide in 1997. Mantovani (2009), in his master's thesis, sought to observe the impact of the National Textbook Program on public education, and presented how the evaluations of the textbook guides were categorized. Let's take a look at some of the data below for the 1997 PNLD.

Chart 2- Categories for classifying textbooks - PNLD 1997

Category	**Characteristics of the work**
Book excluded	Does not meet the minimum requirements; contains problems identified as eliminatory.
Book not recommended	It presents insufficient conditions for the exercise of good education, with improprieties that compromise its effectiveness.
Book recommended with reservations	They have characteristics that meet the minimum quality criteria, but which require attention and supplementation on the part of the teacher.
Recommended book	It fulfills its didactic-pedagogical function and meets the most specific evaluation criteria.

Source: Mantovani (2009)

In this program, 466 textbooks were registered in the areas of Portuguese Language, Mathematics, Science and Social Studies, of which 63 were recommended, 42 were recommended with reservations, 281 were not recommended and 80 were excluded.

In 1997, a new evaluation began for the 1998 PNLD. There were changes to the classification categories and abbreviations and icons were created for classification (MANTOVANI, 2009). Let's look at some of the data below for the 1998 PNLD:

Chart 3- Categories for classifying textbooks - PNLD 1998

Category	**Abbreviation**	**icon**
Book recommended with reservations	RR	*
Recommended book	REC	**
Book recommended with distinction[3]	RD	***

3 The books categorized as recommended with distinction would be those that are very close to the ideal, according to the MEC's criteria.

Source: Mantovani (2009)

In this evaluation, 454 textbooks were submitted in the areas of Literacy, Portuguese Language, Mathematics, Science and Social Studies, of which 19 were recommended with distinction, 47 were recommended, 101 were recommended with reservations, 211 were not recommended and 76 were excluded.

A new evaluation was carried out in 1999 for books from grades 5ª to 8ª , followed by triennial evaluations for each cycle. The textbooks were evaluated by volume and the books were classified as recommended, recommended with reservations and not recommended. After the first survey in 1997, there was an improvement in the quality of the books presented, which led in 1998 to the creation of a new group of books, the so-called recommended with distinction, which were books that had great pedagogical value. (NASCIMENTO, 2011, p. 38).

Another significant change in the evaluation process came about with the 2000 PNLD, when works were no longer evaluated by volumes, but by entire collections.

From 1996 to 2004, the PNLD was able to cover all subjects and encompass all elementary school grades, including the distribution of Portuguese language dictionaries and geographical atlases, with a policy of evaluating, buying and distributing textbooks throughout the country, thus aiming to improve the quality of education in the country through a mechanism considered to be one of the most important in the dissemination of knowledge of a literate culture.

There are also criticisms of the PNLD, including the manipulation of teachers by the publishers of the books approved by the PNLD, in which case teachers often fail to be guided by the Textbook Guide, choosing a proposal convinced by the publishers (MANTOVANI, 2009). The same author points out other obstacles in relation to the PNLD, this time the difficulties faced by publishers who want to have their books included in the PNLD,

> the short period of time between the publication of the notice and the final date for submitting the books for analysis; the impossibility of correcting small technical problems raised during the screening; the lack of a right of defense on the part of the authors and publishers in relation to the results of the evaluations

(MANTOVANI, 2009, p. 76).

However, with the criticisms that have been made, it is worth pointing out that the PNLD has significantly improved the quality of primary school textbooks, given its massive investment in the number of critical readers hired to evaluate the materials, in order to reduce as much as possible the possibility of the book being excluded if it is registered (MANTOVANI, 2009).

Furthermore, it is up to the teacher to participate directly in the process of choosing the textbook, as they are the ones who live directly with the student's reality in the school environment, knowing the specificities that the space brings with it.

CHAPTER 2: MATHEMATICS IN THE TEACHING AND LEARNING PROCESS

2.1 Mathematics: Difficulties and importance in Basic Education

Mathematics, at the most different stages of an individual's schooling, is still characterized today by difficulties on the part of students, which is confirmed by the National Curriculum Parameters: "In our country, mathematics teaching is still marked by high retention rates, the early formalization of concepts, excessive concern with skills training and the mechanization of processes without understanding" (BRASIL, 1998, p.21).

For a long time, it was seen as the "bogeyman" of learning. Students are always afraid to talk about it. There are so many numbers and unknowns that present themselves as a challenge and terrify them. However, even though it is often not learned in the way it should be, Mathematics has evolved over the years and shows its real importance in society. Ponte (2004) considers that in recent decades the teaching of mathematics has undergone many significant changes.

In the 40s and 50s, it was characterized by memorization and mechanization, also known as "traditional teaching". This required students to memorize demonstrations of theorems (memorization) and to practice lists with a huge number of exercises (mechanization). However, the results of this teaching methodology were not significant.

In the 1960s, mathematics curricula underwent a major overhaul, reflecting the international "Modern Mathematics" movement. With a new approach, a new language was introduced, characterized by the symbolism of Logic and Set Theory.

In the 1970s, the abstract and formal were emphasized, without aiming at applications, as a result of new programs developed in the spirit of Modern Mathematics.

In the 1980s, an attempt was made to emphasize the importance of social, anthropological and linguistic aspects, as well as cognitive ones, in learning mathematics. This was in response to the poor results of mathematics learning in previous decades.

In the 1990s, what came to be known as "renewed teaching" emerged, as it was found that it wasn't the calculus tasks that students performed worst on, but rather the more complex tasks that required some reasoning, flexibility and critical thinking.

In Silveira's (2002) view, secondary school math teachers have expressed a sense of blaming the failure of students on teachers in the early grades, because they are unprepared and because they opted for the teaching course because they don't like math and want to get away from it. Thus, the problems that have arisen in relation to the teaching of mathematics at all levels are not new and are presented in a variety of ways and with varying degrees of complexity.

Other reasons that contribute to making learning mathematics even more difficult include the lack of preparation of some teachers, outdated teaching resources and schools with poor infrastructure (FREITAS E SILVA, 2009). In other words, there will be no good learning if the student doesn't feel good and has the need to want to learn, that it makes sense for their life and is related to their culture.

D'Ambrosio (1986) points out that,

> we have to admit, if for no other reason than from a practical point of view, that we talk about the same mathematics everywhere in the world, with the same notation, the same definitions and the same theories, with a few exceptions at a very basic level. At this level, we recognize the existence of mathematical practices that differ essentially from one cultural group to another. At this level, mathematics approaches a variant of the common language, associated with the concept of codification of popular practices and daily needs and the uses of numerical skills. (D'AMBROSIO, 1986, p. 57).

Traditionalism on the part of many teachers is being called into question. The content is often presented with excessive calculations and no importance is given to the objective of calculating. Thus, students apply routine procedures mechanically, which requires little reasoning on their part (CARVALHO, 2005). It is necessary to create new perspectives in relation to calculus, giving meaning to the practice on the part of the teacher.

It is unacceptable for students to feel inferior if they do not develop their learning well, which has led to constant failures. According to Cardoso and Benevides-Pereira

(2009),

> the teacher seems to incorporate the rigor of mathematical knowledge and, in the same way, relates to others around him using the same austerity, contributing to Mathematics being one of the subjects in the school curriculum with one of the highest failure rates. (CARDOSO E BENEVIDES-PEREIRA, 2009, p. 3026).

Despite the difficulties that are almost always imposed on mathematics, it has a lot of relevance, especially in the interaction of human beings with the world in its social and cultural context. The Common Curriculum Base of the State of Pernambuco states that the articulation of mathematics with social practices and needs supports the principle of contextualization (PERNAMBUCO, 2008). According to the document, multiple roles can be attributed to the teaching of mathematics,

> firstly, we should advocate teaching that recognizes the mathematical knowledge and practices of citizens and local communities, which are relatively efficient prerequisite skills, but does not disregard more universal mathematical knowledge. Secondly, it is necessary to develop mathematical skills and abilities that contribute more directly to helping citizens to have a critical view of the society in which they live and to deal with the usual ways of representing numerical indicators of various economic, social and physical phenomena, among others (PERNAMBUCO, 2008, p. 75).

Today there is a need to evolve the knowledge that human beings build. However, it is necessary to interconnect this knowledge with several others. Mathematics will present itself as a model of abstract constructions where a deeper understanding of mathematical models strengthens the contribution of mathematics to other areas of knowledge. In this way, it is possible to overcome an undesirable situation with a view to building citizenship.

2.2 **Mathematics in the final years of elementary school**

Mathematics is a compulsory subject in elementary school curricula, and according to the National Curriculum Parameters its objectives in elementary school are to enable students to,

> identify mathematical knowledge as a means of understanding and transforming the world around them and perceive the intellectual playfulness characteristic of mathematics as an aspect that stimulates interest, curiosity, a spirit of investigation and the development of problem-solving skills; make systematic observations of quantitative and qualitative aspects of reality, establishing interrelationships between them, using mathematical knowledge (arithmetic, geometric, mathematical, algebraic, statistical, combinatorial,

probabilistic); select, organize and produce relevant information in order to interpret and critically evaluate it; solve problem situations, knowing how to validate strategies and results, developing forms of reasoning and processes such as intuition, induction, deduction, analogy, estimation, and using mathematical concepts and procedures, as well as available technological tools; communicate mathematically, i.e. describe, represent and present results accurately and argue about their conjectures, using oral language and establishing relationships between it and different mathematical representations; establish connections between mathematical themes from different fields and between these themes and knowledge from other curricular areas; feeling confident in their own ability to construct mathematical knowledge, developing self-esteem and perseverance in the search for solutions; interacting with their peers in a cooperative way, working collectively to find solutions to proposed problems, identifying aspects that are consensual or not in the discussion of a subject, respecting their colleagues' way of thinking and learning from them (BRASIL, 1998, p. 47).47).

It is possible to see that the responsibilities of those involved in teaching mathematics at this stage will be greater than at the previous stage, as they will now be faced with a completely different learning structure. There will be several subjects, including mathematics, with different teachers and objectives, which will above all require students to adapt to having a certain "independence" in learning.

It is also up to the teacher to be a support at this time for the student, knowing a little about their reality, difficulties and learning. According to the Pernambuco Common Curriculum Base,

this stage of schooling can be seen as a continuation of the previous one, in other words, as an advance, expansion and consolidation of the learning previously achieved. This means that, at this stage, the teacher needs to be well acquainted with what the students have already learned in order to avoid any disruptions that could harm them. (PERNAMBUCO, 2008, p. 93).

At this stage, students will develop resources that are the basis for the knowledge and skills they acquired in the early years of elementary school, so it is necessary to broaden and deepen them, creating knowledge that will help them understand their reality and how they act in it, as well as the possibility of achieving a certain degree of autonomy. Therefore, in addition to the cognitive development of students at this stage, it is important to have observation experiences that indicate relationships between facts and events and also stimulate curiosity and creative ability.

CHAPTER 3 METHODOLOGY

In this chapter, we will detail the methods adopted in order to understand how the research was carried out in its entirety. We used a qualitative approach to the analysis and content analysis as a tool for data collection.

3.1 **Methodological Design**

This study will be carried out through a qualitative analysis, which seeks, among many factors, to understand the phenomena studied. According to Bogdan and Biclen (1994),

> the qualitative research approach requires that the world be examined with the idea that nothing is trivial, that everything has the potential to build a clue that will allow us to establish a more enlightening understanding of our object of study (BOGDAN and BICLEN, 1994, p. 49).

We will check in the critical reviews of the 1999, 2002, 2005, 2008, 2011 and 2014 PNLD Textbook Guides, what the evaluators point out as advances and also criticisms of the two approved collections: *Matemàtica-* Imenes and Lellis and *Matemàtica Idéias e Desafios* - Iracema and Dulce.

We will focus our analysis on the guides through the evaluative synthesis, the description of the work and the analysis of the work, which concisely and comprehensively sets out the details of each work.

In addition to the qualitative approach, the research also looks at content analysis in documents, in our case, textbook guides. This is proposed from the perspective of Bardin (2011) and was first applied in the United States almost half a century ago as an instrument for analyzing communications. According to Santos (2012),

> The technique of content analysis arose from the needs of sociology and psychology. This event was marked by the systematization of the rules and the interest in political symbolism, between 1940 and 1950 in the United States; by the extension of the applications of the technique to different contexts and the emergence of new problems in the methodological field, between 1950 and 1960; and, due to the three phenomena that affected research and content analysis: the use of computers, studies on non-verbal communication and linguistic work, from 1960 to the present day. (SANTOS, 2012, p. 383).

According to Bardin (2011), content analysis allows the conceptualization of knowledge approached through variables inferred by quantitative or qualitative indicators, based on systematic and objective procedures. Thus, he organizes the analysis into three chronological poles:

- Pre-analysis: in which the documents are chosen, hypotheses and objectives for the research are formulated and indicators are developed to support the final interpretation;
- Exploration of the material: in which specific techniques are applied according to the objectives;
- Processing the results: inference and interpretation.

The figure below shows the stages of content analysis in more detail.

Figurei: Schematic summary of the development of a content analysis

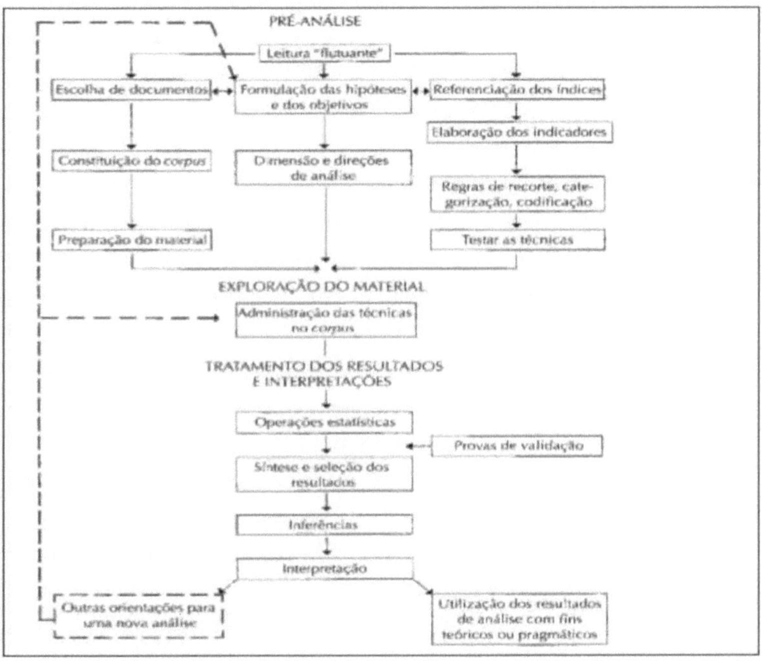

Source: Bardin, 2011, p.132.

From the perspective of content analysis, categorization becomes a necessary procedure for carrying out the analysis. Thus, Bardin (2011) reports that,

categorization is an operation of classifying the constituent elements of a set by differentiating them and then regrouping them according to genre (analogy), using previously defined criteria. Categories are headings or classes which bring together a group of elements (recording units) under a generic heading, grouped according to the common characteristics of these elements (BARDIN, 2011, p. 147).

The last six Mathematics Textbook Guides approved in the 1999, 2002, 2005, 2008, 2011 and 2014 PNLD for Elementary School II were chosen for categorization and analysis. Their references are listed below:

- BRASIL. **PNLD 1999 Textbook Guide:** Mathematics. Brasilia: MEC, 1998.
- . **PNLD 2002 Textbook Guide:** Mathematics. Brasilia: MEC, 2001.
- . **PNLD 2005 Textbook Guide:** Mathematics. Brasilia: MEC, 2004.
- . **PNLD 2008 Textbook Guide:** Mathematics. Brasilia: MEC, 2007.
- . **PNLD 2011 Textbook Guide:** Mathematics. Ministry of Education. Available at: <http://www.mec.gov.br> Accessed on: Aug. 18, 2015.
- . **PNLD 2014 Textbook Guide:** Mathematics. Ministry of Education. Available at: <http://www.mec.gov.br> Accessed on: Aug. 18, 2015.

Thus, with the help of the Textbook Guides themselves, units of analysis were created and the categories associated with them were defined, as follows:

Table 4: categorizations

Units of analysis	Categories
Selection and distribution of content	1- Covering the five fields of mathematics (numbers and operations, algebra and functions, geometry, quantities and measures, statistics and probability) 2- Distribution and articulation of fields and contents
Content approach	1- Content approach in the field: Numbers and operations 2- Content approach in the field: Algebra and functions 3- Approach to content in the field: Geometry

	4- Content approach in the field: Quantities and measures 5- Approach to content in the field: Statistics and probability
Teaching-learning methodology	1- Methodology in the student-context relationship 2- Methodology in the relationship of interaction with individuals 3- Methodology in the use of teaching resources and extra activities
Teacher's manual	1- - Theoretical foundation of the collection 2- Guidelines for using the book 3- Suggestions for extra activities, specific assessments and training

Source: Author, 2015

We note above the creation of four units of analysis, subdivided with their respective categories, which total thirteen. We will analyze all of them based on the Textbook Guides through the evaluative synthesis, description of the work and analysis of the work.

CHAPTER 4. ANALYSIS AND DISCUSSION

The aim of this chapter is to present, discuss and analyze the data obtained through content analysis, explored in the 1999, 2002, 2005, 2008, 2011 and 2014 Textbook Guides using a qualitative approach.

4.1 **Analysis path**

In accordance with the content analysis approach described by Bardin (2011), we began the first stage by choosing the material to be used, in our case the Textbook Guides. This was followed by the exploration of the material, in which the techniques for analysis were applied, and finally the treatment of the results, i.e. the actual analysis in the sub-item below.

4.1.2 **Data analysis**

PNLD 1999[4]

Mathematics - Imenes and Lellis

Content selection and distribution

- Covering the five fields of mathematics (numbers and operations, algebra and functions, geometry, quantities and measures, statistics and probability).

In the 5th grade book[a] the subjects covered are: Numbers and operations, Geometry, Quantities and measures, Statistics and Probability. In the 6th grade (7th year) the subjects covered are from the fields: Numbers and operations, Geometry, Quantities and measures, Statistics and Probability. In the 7th grade (8th year) the subjects covered are from the fields: Numbers and operations, Geometry, Algebra, Statistics and Probability. In the 8th grade (9th year) the subjects covered are from the fields: Numbers and operations, Geometry, Algebra, Statistics and Probability.

- Distribution and articulation of fields and contents

In all the volumes (5[a] to 8[a]), the subjects in each field are presented in a correct and

4 In this PNLD, the analysis was done by series

graded way, linked to each other and to other areas of knowledge. One of the book's great merits is that the content is presented through problem situations.

Content approach

- Content approach in the field: Numbers and operations

In all volumes (5th to 8th grade), mental calculation and estimation activities are encouraged. The 5th grade book covers topics such as: Fundamental operations - natural numbers, multiples, divisors, inverse operations, potentiation, fractions, operations with fractions, equivalence. In the 6th grade book, subjects such as negative numbers are covered, while fractions and decimal numbers are taken up again. In the 7th grade book, subjects such as: prime numbers; fractions, decimal numbers, inverse operations, division of fractions and mmc are resumed. The 8th grade book includes mental calculation and estimation activities, problem formulation and observing regularities.

- Content approach in the field: Algebra and functions

In the 5th grade book, algebra is not dealt with directly, but the idea of letters is used in some problems. The 6th grade book does not deal directly with algebra, but gradually introduces expressions from Portuguese into algebraic language, as well as simple calculations and problems to be solved by equations. In the 7th grade book, algebra is emphasized through activities with variables, unknowns, formulas and equations, and subjects such as 1st degree equations and systems of 1st degree equations are worked on. In the 8th grade book, algebra is developed more rigorously, with examples of not only 1st degree equations but also 2nd degree equations and systems of equations; the notion of functions is covered through the content of simple interest and the rule of three.

- Approach to content in the field: Geometry

The 5th grade book[a] covers subjects such as: spatial and flat figures, symmetry and geometric constructions. The 6th grade book encourages the use of geometric tools such as the tangram and covers topics such as: geometric constructions, determining angles, calculating areas, classifying geometric shapes. The 7th grade book covers subjects such as: spatial and flat figures, symmetry, geometric constructions, proportionality, calculating areas; as well as subjects such as planning and constructing spatial figures. The 8th grade book covers subjects such as: similarity, trigonometry, measurements (area and volume of geometric and plane figures), geometric constructions.

- Content approach in the field: Quantities and measures

The 5th grade book covers subjects such as: decimal numbers (standardized units of length, area and mass). The 6th grade book covers topics such as: proportionality (map scale, similar figures and concepts of speed and area). The 7th grade book does not cover the topic of quantities and measures. The 8th grade textbook does not cover the topic of quantities and measures.

- Approach to content in the field: Statistics and probability

The 5th grade book covers subjects such as: analysis of possibilities and reading and interpreting graphs. In the 6th grade textbook, the concepts of statistics and probability, and the construction and interpretation of graphs are taken up in greater depth. In the 7th grade book, the content is taken up again and further developed with the introduction of the notion of chance and sample and graphs with curved lines. In the 8th grade book, the content is taken up again and the relationship between probability and the notion of sample is explored in greater depth.

Teaching-learning methodology

- Methodology in the student-context relationship

In the collection, students work on the content through problem situations. They are challenged by creative, original and engaging activities, as well as diversified experiences in rich and varied learning contexts.

- Methodology in the relationship of interaction with individuals

In the collection, the students' relationship with other classmates is stimulated through a section called *Action,* where activities are developed with games, stimulating in pairs or larger groups.

- Methodology in the use of didactic resources and extra activities

It is not clear how the student should use the extra resources and/or activities, but it is suggested in the teacher's manual.

Teacher's manual

- Theoretical foundation of the collection

In the manual, the authors justify the need for changes in math teaching, both in terms of content and teaching methodology.

- Guidelines for using the book

This collection lists considerations about mathematics and how to work with it, as well as suggested lesson plans.

- Suggestions for extra activities, specific assessments and training

The manual presents and analyzes teaching resources such as: newspapers and magazines, electronic devices, plastic arts, the use of educational books, the use of calculators, computers and videos. It also discusses the importance of continuous and diversified assessment.

Mathematics: Ideas and Challenges - Iracema and Dulce

Content selection and distribution

- Covering the five fields of mathematics (numbers and operations, algebra and functions, geometry, quantities and measures, statistics and probability).

In the 5th grade book[a] the subjects covered are: Numbers and operations, Geometry, Quantities and measures. In the 6th grade book (7th year) the subjects covered are: Numbers and operations, Geometry, Algebra and functions. In the 7th grade book (8th year) the subjects covered are from the fields: Numbers and operations, Geometry, Algebra and functions. In the 8th grade book, the subjects covered are: Numbers and operations, algebra and functions, geometry, statistics and probability.

- Distribution of fields in conjunction with other areas of knowledge

In all the volumes (5th to 8th grade), there is a lack of integration between the fields of Numbers and Operations, Geometry, Algebra and Quantities and Measures. There is also a greater emphasis on the formulation of problems and open questions.

Content approach

- Content approach in the field: Numbers and operations

The 5th grade book takes up subjects such as: natural numbers, through a historical view; addition, subtraction, multiplication, division are explored through problem situations; new subjects are also covered such as: potentiation, radication, divisibility, with a geometric approach and by decomposition; MMC and MDC, treated without attention to understanding; fractions, well developed, but without the meanings of ratio and operator; absolute rational numbers; decimal numbers and operations are treated adequately, but there is no justification of the algorithms for multiplying and dividing decimals. The 6th grade book covers new subjects such as: Integers, approached in an appropriate way, do not insist on the set Z; operations with integers, addition and subtraction are carried out in a contextualized way, while multiplication and division are done in a more traditional way, potentiation and radication are done using scientific notation; Rational numbers are carefully represented geometrically and using scientific notation. In the 7th grade textbook, subjects such as: Real numbers are introduced through decimals and the extraction of the square root. In the 8th grade book, subjects such as: Potentiation, worked on through problem situations; Radication; Radicals and operations were overemphasized.

- Content approach in the field: Algebra and functions

The 5[a] grade book does not cover algebra and functions. In the 6th grade textbook,[a] , the following content is covered: first-degree equations with one unknown, integrated with geometry and measurements; Inequations, introduced through problem situations integrated with geometry; systems of first-degree equations with two unknowns; Percentage and simple interest in the functions section, covered using graphs with problems from society. The 7th grade textbook covers the following topics: algebraic calculation, integrated with geometry and measurements; notable products; it also covers polynomials and algebraic fractions, but due to the grade the emphasis is unnecessary; equations are taken up and deepened; systems of equations are adequate, but the geometric solutions of problems and exercises are not emphasized. The 8th grade textbook covers the following topics: Second-degree equations, which are given a traditional treatment on the first few pages; Systems of second-degree equations and irrational equations are given less emphasis; Functions.

- Approach to content in the field: Geometry

The 5th grade textbook deals with geometry, areas and volumes, where manipulation of figures is presented, but is developed without innovation. The 6th grade textbook covers geometry correctly, but there is a lack of clarity regarding the concept of area; ratios and proportions, proportionality, integrating geometry and everyday situations. The 7th grade textbook deals with geometry, where it is taken up in the traditional way; parallel lines are dealt with in the traditional way; circumferences begin with situations from the student's life and are then dealt with traditionally. The 8th grade textbook deals with the content of: Ratios and segments, presented in an interesting way through the reduction of one figure into another similar one; Thales' theorem; Similarities are introduced through applications and reduction of figures; Metric relations, Pythagoras' theorems and trigonometric relations are presented in the traditional way.

- Content approach in the field: Quantities and measures

In the 5th grade textbook[a] the content of the system of measures is dealt with, where interesting situations are presented, but there is no integration with other axes. In the 6th, 7th and 8th grade books, the field of quantities and measures is not covered.

- Approach to content in the field: Statistics and probability

In the 5th, 6th and 7th grade textbooks, statistics and probability are not covered. Only in the 8th grade textbook is the field of statistics dealt with, but in the last chapter and in the form of an appendix.

Teaching-learning methodology

- Methodology in the student-context relationship

The collection takes into account the student's experience and seeks to stimulate the rediscovery of concepts and the apprehension of meanings through varied activities. The subjects are triggered by problem situations.

- Methodology in the relationship of interaction with individuals (classmates and teacher) It is not made clear how students should interact with other individuals.

- Methodology in the use of didactic resources and extra activities

The collection encourages them to use extra activities such as challenges and games in the *Reading* section.

Teacher's manual

- Theoretical foundation of the collection

In the collection, the theoretical assumptions of the proposal are not clearly explained, but there is a concern to get away from the traditional line, and there is coherence between the objectives to be achieved and those that can be achieved through the use of the book.

- Guidelines for using the book

There is no clear guidance on how teachers should use the book.

- Suggestions for extra activities, specific assessments and training.

In the collection, although summarized, the methodological indications and comments on each of the contents are useful for teachers and can contribute to their training and updating. The text on assessment in Mathematics, although also very brief, is of good quality and can help teachers.

Comparative analysis of the collections - PNLD 1999

It was possible to see from the categorizations in this guide that in terms of the scope of the fields of Mathematics, both collections present the five fields of Mathematics throughout the series. However, the collection *Matemàtica Ideias e Desafios - Iracema e Dulce*, places greater emphasis on the fields of Numbers and Operations, Algebra and Functions and Geometry, leading to a lack of integration between the other fields. This is noticeable in the fields of Quantities and Measures, where content from this field is only covered in the 5th grade book[a] and in the field of Statistics and Probability, where the content is covered in the 8th grade book and in the form of an appendix. The *Mathematics - Imenes and Lellis* collection*, on* the other hand, presents the opposite - in addition to a good articulation between the fields, the contents are presented through problem situations.

In the teaching and learning methodology, both in the student-context relationship and in the relationship of interaction with individuals, the collection *Matemàtica - Imenes and Lellis,* presents in a clear and objective way how the collection interferes in this methodological process, only in the methodology in the use of didactic resources and extra activities that is not exposed how this methodology should be. In the collection *Matemàtica Ideias e Desafios - Iracema e Dulce,* the methodology of interacting with individuals is not brought to the student's attention, but it does present contextualized problem situations.

As for the teacher's manual in the collection *Matemàtica - Imenes and Lellis,* the authors express the theoretical basis of the collection through the need for changes in mathematics teaching, in the guidelines for using the book, lesson plans are suggested and suggestions are given for both assessment and the use of teaching resources. In the collection *Matemàtica Ideias e Desafios - Iracema e Dulce,* the theoretical assumptions are not made explicit, nor is there any guidance on how to use the book, but there is a concern to get away from the traditional line by briefly addressing indications and comments for teacher training.

***PNLD 2002*[5]**

5 From this guide, the books are evaluated by collection.

Mathematics - Imenes and Lellis

Content selection and distribution

- Covering the five fields of mathematics (numbers and operations, algebra and functions, geometry, quantities and measures, statistics and probability).

The five fields of mathematics appear throughout the collection, highlighting the treatment of information in all grades and little emphasis on technical content such as algebraic calculation, as well as avoiding others such as biquadratic equations and irrationals.

- Distribution and articulation of fields and contents

The collection is compatible with the proposal of a spiral curriculum, as the mathematical topics are dealt with in successive stages, throughout the grades, in progressive degrees of length and complexity. The fields are integrated in various parts of the collection.

Content approach[6]

- Content approach in the field: Numbers and operations

The contents are presented in the same way as in the 1999 PNLD, but in the 8ª grade book the contents appear: numbers and calculations and classifying numbers.

- Content approach in the field: Algebra and functions

The contents are presented in the same way as the 1999 PNLD.

- Approach to content in the field: Geometry

The content is presented in the same way as in the 1999 PNLD, but in the 6th grade book, the proportionality, area and volume content that was previously in the 7th and 8th grade books is presented as new content.

- Approach to content in the field: Quantities and measures

---

6 As a practical matter, the categories of the unit of analysis from this PNLD onwards: approach to the content will be explained by means of the content that has changed or is presented as new in the evaluation based on the previous PNLD.

The contents are presented in the same way as the 1999 PNLD.

- Approach to content in the field: Statistics and probability

The content is presented in the same way as in the 1999 PNLD, but it can be seen that the idea of Probability is emphasized more in all grades in the 1999 PNLD.

Teaching-learning methodology

- Methodology in the student-context relationship

The discussion of content promoted by the section *Conversing about the text* and the stimulus to *the* expression of the debate of ideas, in the sections *Action in* particular, are constant throughout the book.

- Methodology in the relationship of interaction with individuals (colleagues and teacher)

Encouraging teamwork and student-student interaction is an aspect that contributes to training for social coexistence and citizenship.

- Methodology in the use of didactic resources and extra activities

The *Action* section offers research, games and mediation activities.

Teacher's manual

- Theoretical foundation of the collection

In the collection, there is an indication of a complementary bibliography and a list of associations and centers of Mathematics Education that can contribute to the teacher's updating.

- Guidelines for using the book

The manual explains the theoretical-methodological assumptions underlying the production of the book, provides guidance for teachers on how to use it and discusses the organization of the content covered, including suggested lesson plans and forms of assessment.

- Suggestions for extra activities, specific assessments and training.

The development of the content and the elements of assessment are presented in an articulated manner and, in addition to general considerations, suggest specific questions for many of the topics covered.

Mathematics: Ideas and Challenges - Iracema and Dulce

Content selection and distribution

- Covering the five fields of mathematics (numbers and operations, algebra and functions, geometry, quantities and measures, statistics and probability).

In the collection, the five fields of mathematics predominate, but there is no integration between them.

- Distribution and articulation of fields and contents

The collection presents innovative curricular content proposals, but there is a reduced frequency of some of the content, and the notions of statistics can only be found in the last chapter of the 8ª series, there is also a

the study of numbers and operations is concentrated in the 5th and 6th grade textbooks, algebra and geometry in the 7th grade and geometry in the 8th grade. Emphasis is placed on very technical subjects such as algebraic calculus in the 7th grade textbook and calculus with radicals in the 8th grade textbook, thus not keeping up with the most up-to-date curricular trends.

Content approach

- Content approach in the field: Numbers and operations

The contents are presented in the same way as the 1999 PNLD.

- Content approach in the field: Algebra and functions The content is presented in the same way as in the 1999 PNLD.

- Approach to content in the field: Geometry

The contents are presented in the same way as in the 1999 PNLD, but the contents of angles and polygons are new in the 5th grade book and in the 7th grade book, the sum of the angles of a triangle, polygons, triangles, quadrilaterals and circles.

- Content approach in the field: Quantities and measures The content is presented in the same way as the 1999 PNLD.

- Approach to content in the field: Statistics and probability

The contents are presented in the same way as the 1999 PNLD.

Teaching-learning methodology

- Methodology in the student-context relationship

The content is presented in a logical and linear sequence, so when a subject is introduced, the content that will support it has already been introduced. It can also be seen that the exercises and problems only seek to apply and deepen, without encouraging students to discover new meanings, and that the content is systematized quickly, with an excessive amount of information, thus not contributing to the student's mental action. However, one of the positive aspects of the book is the presentation of contextualized problem situations.

- Methodology in the relationship of interaction with individuals (classmates and teacher) It is not made clear how students should interact with other individuals.

- Methodology in the use of didactic resources and extra activities

In the collection, they are encouraged to use extra activities such as challenges and games in the *Free Section.*

Teacher's manual

- Theoretical foundation of the collection

In the collection, the theoretical foundations of the proposal are not clearly explained in the work's methodological choices.

- Guidelines for using the book

The teacher's manual provides brief guidelines for teachers.

- Suggestions for extra activities, specific assessments and training

In the *Evaluation* section, there are concepts and suggestions for procedures on this subject and two more with bibliographical suggestions.

Comparative analysis of collections - PNLD 2002

In this guide, it was possible to see that in terms of the scope of the fields of mathematics, the two collections continue to present the five fields of mathematics throughout the grades. However, the collection *Matemàtica Ideias e Desafios - Iracema e Dulce,* continues to focus on the study of numbers and operations in the books for grades 5ª and 6ª , algebra and geometry in grade 7ª and geometry in grade 8ª , Emphasis on very technical subjects such as algebraic calculus in the 7th grade textbook and calculus with radicals in the 8th grade textbook, and notions of statistics again only in the last chapter of the 8th grade, thus not keeping up with the most up-to-date curricular trends. The *Mathematics - Imenes and Lellis* collection, on the other hand, continues to show the opposite, with good integration between the fields, an emphasis on the treatment of information in all grades and little emphasis on technical content such as algebraic calculation.

In the *Mathematics - Imenes and Lellis* collection*, the* teaching-learning methodology, in the student-context relationship, promotes discussion of the content through the sections *Talking about the text and Action,* the relationship of interaction with individuals is stimulated through teamwork and class discussions, and the methodology of using teaching resources and extra activities appears in this guide from the *Action* section onwards. In the collection *Matemàtica Ideias e Desafios - Iracema and Dulce,* the methodology of interacting with individuals is still not emphasized for the student's knowledge, but contextualized problem situations continue to be presented.

As for the teacher's manual in the collection *Matemàtica - Imenes and Lellis,* there is an indication of a complementary bibliography, the teacher is instructed on how to use the book, the organization of the content covered is discussed, and lesson plans and forms of assessment are suggested. In the collection *Matemàtica Ideias e Desafios - Iracema e Dulce,* the theoretical assumptions are still not made explicit, but this guide provides brief guidance on how to use the book and the origin of the *Assessment* section, which discusses conceptions and suggested procedures on this subject.

PNLD 2005

Mathematics - Imenes and Lellis

Content selection and distribution

- Covering the five fields of mathematics (numbers and operations, algebra and functions, geometry, quantities and measures, statistics and probability).

The five fields of mathematics appear throughout the collection, highlighting the study of geometry, especially symmetry, perspectives and projections and geometric constructions with instruments.

- Distribution and articulation of fields and contents

The content is covered, taken up again, expanded and deepened, and presented in meaningful, contextualized and unnatural situations. It presents various approaches, making it a good proposal for organizing the curriculum in a spiral. The content is articulated, as themes from the fields of mathematics are often revisited in connection with new ones.

Content approach

- Content approach in the field: Numbers and operations

The contents are presented in the same way as the PNLD 2002

- Content approach in the field: Algebra and functions

The content is presented in the same way as in the 2002 PNLD, but in this PNLD the equations content is dealt with in the 6th grade book[a] , whereas in the other evaluations it was in the 7th grade book, and the trigonometry content appears in this evaluation.

- Approach to content in the field: Geometry

The content is presented in the same way as in the 2002 PNLD, but in this PNLD, the 6th, 7th and 8th grade textbooks deal with three-dimensional, experimental and deductive geometry.

- Content approach in the field: Quantities and measures

The content is presented in the same way as in the 2002 PNLD, but includes maps and location.

- Approach to content in the field: Statistics and probability

The contents are presented in the same way as the PNLD 2002.

Teaching-learning methodology

- Methodology in the student-context relationship

Discussion of the content is promoted by the section *Talking about the text*, with questions designed to encourage students to express their thoughts and exchange ideas.

- Methodology in the relationship of interaction with individuals (colleagues and teacher)

The book assumes that classroom activities are centered on student participation, whether in individual or group work, or in class discussions.

- Methodology in the use of didactic resources and extra activities

The *Action* section proposes activities with games and auxiliary materials, as well as the collection's frequent request to use drawing instruments, calculators and educational software.

Teacher's manual

- Theoretical foundation of the collection

The supplement *Pedagogical advice* in the handbook contains sections such as: comments on teaching mathematics, proposals on assessment, guidelines for developing the content, answers to and comments on the questions, sources for updating and improving teachers.

- Guidelines for using the book

The recommendations and guidelines contained in the manual help to ensure that the collection is used properly in the teaching-learning process. Its suggestions and theoretical and methodological reflections can help to update teachers.

- Suggestions for extra activities, specific assessments and training

Assessment is seen as a way of promoting learning, guiding teaching action and helping the student. In this sense, there are suggestions for various instruments, such as self-assessment, observations of student work in class, notebook observations, tests, essays, surveys, portfolios and paradidatic readings.

Mathematics: Ideas and Challenges - Iracema and Dulce

Content selection and distribution

- Covering the five fields of mathematics (numbers and operations, algebra and functions, geometry, quantities and measures, statistics and probability).

The five fields of mathematics predominate in the collection, incorporating important topics in information processing (statistics, combinatorics) and geometry (geometric transformations in the plane). Mathematics topics are linked to other areas of knowledge.

- Distribution and articulation of fields and contents

There is an adequate distribution of topics. However, there is a tendency for topics to be concentrated at certain points in the collection, such as the study of numbers: in the 6th grade book[a] , integers are presented and covered in two chapters. Operations with negative rational numbers are only covered in one chapter, which reflects a linear organization of the mathematics curriculum. The activities emphasize algebraic calculation with the fixation of rules and formulas, with little emphasis on the ability to argue.

Content approach

- Content approach in the field: Numbers and operations

The contents are presented in the same way as the PNLD 2002, but decimal numbers are not included in the 7th grade book.

- Content approach in the field: Algebra and functions

The content is presented in the same way as in the 2002 PNLD, but inequalities are not included in the 6th grade book.

- Approach to content in the field: Geometry

The content is presented in the same way as in the 2002 PNLD, but angles, circles and circumference will begin to be covered in the 6th grade book and patterns and movements in geometry in the 7th grade book.

- Approach to content in the field: Quantities and measures

The content is presented in the same way as in the 2002 PNLD, but in this PNLD proportionality, ratios and proportions are dealt with in the 6ª grade book.

- Approach to content in the field: Statistics and probability

The content is presented in the same way as in the 2002 PNLD, but in this PNLD the field of statistics is introduced in the 7th grade book.

Teaching-learning methodology

- Methodology in the student-context relationship

The content is presented on the basis of problem situations, contextualization and interesting approaches in a linear organization, which means that many subjects are exhausted in a single chapter or series. A positive feature of the book is the efficient systematization and organization of the concepts. There is also a concern with the acquisition of calculation procedures and techniques, often prioritizing these skills to the detriment of understanding meanings.

- Methodology in the relationship of interaction with individuals (classmates and teacher) It is not made clear how students should interact with other individuals.

- Methodology in the use of didactic resources and extra activities

The collection encourages the use of extra activities such as challenges and games in the *Free Section,* as well as stimulating the manipulation and construction of geometric solids and activities that explore tangram, origami and pentamino. The use of calculators is also encouraged.

Teacher's manual

- Theoretical foundation of the collection

The teacher's manual contains a pedagogical supplement that presents theoretical assumptions.

- Guidelines for using the book

The teacher's manual reproduces the student's book, with answers to the activities, and offers methodological and didactic guidance.

- Suggestions for extra activities, specific assessments and training

The teacher's manual contains a pedagogical supplement that presents Mathematics assessment, indications for continuing teacher training and indications for further reading and activity development.

Comparative analysis of collections - PNLD 2005

The scope of the fields of Mathematics in the two collections continues to be presented throughout the grades in all five fields. However, the collection *Matemàtica Ideias e Desafios - Iracema e Dulce,* continues to concentrate topics at some points in the collection, such as the study of numbers, in the 6th grade book[a] , integers are presented and exhausted in two chapters, operations with negative rational numbers are covered in only one chapter, which reflects a linear organization of the mathematics curriculum, and the activities emphasize algebraic calculation with the fixation of rules and formulas, with little emphasis on the ability to argue. The collection *Matemàtica-Imenes e Lellis,* on the other hand, continues to articulate content with themes from the fields of mathematics, often taken up in connection with new ones.

In the *Mathematics - Imenes and Lellis* collection*, the* teaching-learning methodology, in the student-context relationship, continues to discuss the content in the section *Talking about the text,* the relationship of interaction with individuals is stimulated through teamwork and the methodology in the use of teaching resources and extra activities continues in this guide in the *Action* section. In the collection *Matemàtica Ideias e Desafios - Iracema e Dulce,* the methodology of interacting with individuals is still not emphasized for the student's knowledge, but it continues to present content with contextualized problem situations and the stimulation of challenges and games in the *Free Section.*

As for the teacher's handbook in the collection *Matemàtica - Imenes and Lellis, there* is the supplement *Assessoria pedagògica (Pedagogical advice*) which presents sections such as: comments on the teaching of mathematics, a proposal on assessment, guidelines for developing the content, answers to and comments on the questions, sources for updating and improving teachers. In the collection *Matemàtica Ideias e Desafios - Iracema e Dulce*, the theoretical assumptions, assessment in mathematics, suggestions for continuing teacher training, further reading and the development of activities in this guide are presented in a pedagogical supplement, and the manual also offers didactic and methodological guidelines.

PNLD 2008

Mathematics - Imenes and Lellis

Content selection and distribution

- Covering the five fields of mathematics (numbers and operations, algebra and functions, geometry, quantities and measures, statistics and probability).

The five fields of mathematics appear throughout the collection. Geometry stands out with the study of spatial location, views and perspectives, and the introduction to financial mathematics is well contextualized in the world of work.

- Distribution and articulation of fields and contents

The content is based on a variety of contextualized problem situations which challenge the student and make the most of their prior knowledge. Texts in mother tongue, figures, tables, graphs, diagrams and mathematical symbols are appropriately integrated. Numeracy is taught in grades 5^a and 6^a , while algebra is taught more in the final grades. The fields of information processing, quantities and measures and geometry are well distributed and there is integration between the last two. One of the main features of the book is the articulation between the various fields of mathematics.

Content approach

- Content approach in the field: Numbers and operations

The content is presented in the same way as in the 2005 PNLD, but in this PNLD negative numbers begin to be covered in the 5th grade book.

- Content approach in the field: Algebra and functions

The content is presented in the same way as in the 2005 PNLD, but in this PNLD, the 5th grade book starts with percentages, the 7th grade book includes factoring and the product of polynomials and the 8th grade book includes the perfect square trinomial.

- Approach to content in the field: Geometry

The contents are presented in the same way as in the 2005 PNLD, but in this PNLD they are covered in the book for grade 5ª : primes and pyramids, views, cylinders, spheres, cones, maps.

- Content approach in the field: Quantities and measures

The contents are presented in the same way as in the 2005 PNLD, but in this PNLD this field is not covered in the 8th grade book.

- Approach to content in the field: Statistics and probability

The contents are presented in the same way as the PNLD 2005.

Teaching-learning methodology

- Methodology in the student-context relationship

The collection features the section *Conversing with the text*, which presents the content to be worked on and activities for the classroom and home. Most of the time, the student is asked to systematize the subject studied rather than receiving it ready-made.

- Methodology in the relationship of interaction with individuals (colleagues and teacher)

The *Action* sections encourage students to work in pairs or small groups. The methodology adopted contributes to interaction between students, who are encouraged to work in small groups.

- Methodology in the use of didactic resources and extra activities Students are often instructed to look in the mathematical dictionary for definitions that are not included in the main body of the text.

Teacher's manual

- Theoretical foundation of the collection

The textbook's *pedagogical advisory* service provides an excellent support structure for teachers using the collection. Its theoretical foundation is based on national curriculum documents and recent ideas on the teaching and learning of mathematics.

- Guidelines for using the book

The handbook discusses various situations and presents guidelines for each chapter of the student's book, which can contribute to the intended teaching actions.

- Suggestions for extra activities, specific assessments and training

There are also suggestions for extra activities and specific assessments, as well as information on interdisciplinary work and the use of new information and communication technologies.

Mathematics: Ideas and Challenges - Iracema and Dulce

Content selection and distribution

- Covering the five fields of mathematics (numbers and operations, algebra and functions, geometry, quantities and measures, statistics and probability).

In the collection, the five fields of mathematics predominate. There is a balance between practical situations and formalization, but there is a lot of concern with the use of the symbolic language of mathematics, from the 5th grade onwards[a] to the detriment of the mathematical object.

- Distribution and articulation of fields and contents

The book shows a certain imbalance in the distribution of content. There is an emphasis on the fields of numbers and operations, algebra and geometry to the detriment of topics on quantities and measures and information processing. Despite this, the subjects are interspersed, which makes it easier to connect the fields. The collection values the articulation between new and previously covered knowledge, but uses definitions that have not been worked on before.

Content approach

- Content approach in the field: Numbers and operations

The contents are presented in the same way as the PNLD 2005.

- Content approach in the field: Algebra and functions

The content is presented in the same way as in the 2005 PNLD, but in this PNLD percentages are covered in the 5th grade book and trigonometry in the 8th grade book.

- Approach to content in the field: Geometry

[a] The content is presented in the same way as in the 2005 PNLD, but the 7th grade book covers: perpendicular lines, right-angled triangles and their roots, circles and circumferences, and the 8th grade book covers: circles and circumferences, relative positions.

- Approach to content in the field: Quantities and measures

The contents are presented in the same way as the 2005 PNLD.

- Approach to content in the field: Statistics and probability

The content is presented in the same way as in the 2005 PNLD, but in this PNLD statistics begins to be covered in the 5th and 6th grade textbooks in the content of fractions, whole numbers and equations.

Teaching-learning methodology

- Methodology in the student-context relationship

The themes are approached on the basis of situations in which they are used. This is done by means of a text which includes one or more activities, allowing the student to participate actively. This is followed by sections with activities and exercises to help students grasp and apply the theory, with more complex problems and some of which have been solved.

- Methodology in the relationship of interaction with individuals (classmates and teacher) Unlike other assessments, special sections stand out, such as *Exchange ideas and solve* with activities involving groups or the whole class, thus encouraging active participation by students and the socialization of knowledge.

- Methodology in the use of didactic resources and extra activities

The collection encourages the use of extra activities such as games in the *Free section.* The use of calculators is also encouraged.

Teacher's manual

- Theoretical basis of the collection

The teacher's manual explains the collection's guidelines and contributes to the teacher's classroom practice.

- Guidelines for using the book

Although brief, the didactic guidelines and in-depth texts contained in the manual are very important for those who do not have other sources of information.

- Suggestions for extra activities, specific assessments and training

The manual discusses assessment in mathematics and offers suggestions for continuing teacher training. It also encourages teachers to look in newspapers and magazines for materials on the topics they will be studying and suggests that work with these materials be expanded, depending on the needs and interests of the students.

Comparative analysis of collections - PNLD 2008

The five fields of mathematics in the two collections continue to be presented throughout the grades. However, the collection *Matemàtica Ideias e Desafios - Iracema and Dulce,* continues to show a certain imbalance in the distribution of content, emphasizing the fields of numbers and operations, algebra and geometry to the detriment of the topics of quantities and measures and information processing, although in this guide the subjects are interspersed, which facilitates the articulation between the fields. The *Mathematics - Imenes and Lellis* collection, on the other hand, continues to articulate content between the fields of mathematics, as well as various contextualized problem situations.

In the collection *Matemàtica - Imenes and Lellis, in* terms of teaching and learning methodology, the student-context relationship continues with the discussion of the content through the section *Conversando sobre o texto (Talking about the text),* the relationship of interaction with individuals is stimulated through the section *Açâo (Action*) and the methodology in the use of didactic resources and extra activities is encouraged, such as the use of mathematical dictionaries. In the collection *Matemàtica Ideias e Desafios - Iracema e Dulce,* the methodology of interacting with individuals, unlike the previous guides, is emphasized in the special sections such as *Troque ideias e resolva* with activities involving groups or the whole class, the *Free Section* with games, and the themes are approached based on situations in which they are used.

As for the teacher's manual in the collection *Matemàtica - Imenes and Lellis,* the supplement *Assessoria pedagògica* continues, there are also guidelines for each chapter of the student's book and the inclusion of suggestions for extra activities and specific assessments. In the collection *Matemàtica Ideias e Desafios - Iracema e Dulce,* the manual explains the collection's guidelines, presents didactic guidelines, although they are brief, points out issues of continuing teacher training and also discusses assessment in mathematics.

PNLD 2011

Mathematics - Imenes and Lellis

Content selection and distribution

- Covering the five fields of mathematics (numbers and operations, algebra and functions, geometry, quantities and measures, statistics and probability).

The five fields of mathematics appear throughout the collection. Less common subjects at this stage of education are focused on, such as the different types of symmetry and the volume of a cylinder.

- Distribution and articulation of fields and contents

The topics are not covered in one go, but are taken up, deepened and expanded, sometimes in the same book, sometimes in books from later years. The distribution of the fields is appropriate, in each book and throughout the volumes. The book presents significant links between different fields in the texts and activities.

To better visualize how the fields for each year in this collection are distributed, we have inserted a graph provided by the 2011 Textbook Guide.

Graph 1: Distribution of the fields of Mathematics in the Matemàtica collection

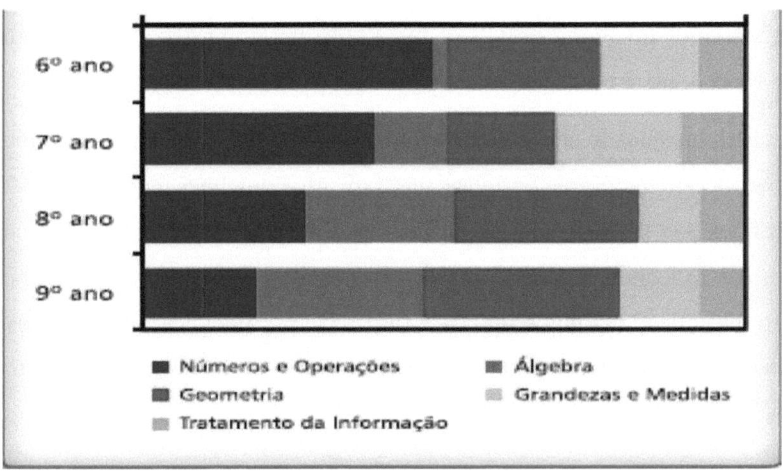

Source: Textbook Guide, 2011

Content approach

- Content approach in the field: Numbers and operations

The contents are presented in the same way as the PNLD 2008.

- Content approach in the field: Algebra and functions The content is presented in the same way as in the 2008 PNLD.

- Approach to content in the field: Geometry

The contents are presented in the same way as the PNLD 2008.

- Content approach in the field: Quantities and measures

The content is presented in the same way as in the 2008 PNLD, but in this PNLD the content of measures is dealt with in the 8ª grade book.

- Approach to content in the field: Statistics and probability The content is presented in the same way as the PNLD 2008.

Teaching-learning methodology

- Methodology in the student-context relationship

In the book, the exploration of mathematical texts always starts with questions to be discussed orally, which are presented in the section *Talking about the text*. Sometimes the students themselves are asked, even at this point, to make partial formalizations of the concepts and procedures being studied.

- Methodology in the relationship of interaction with individuals (classmates and teacher) Há activities proposed to be done individually or in groups. The section called *Action* mainly includes investigations to be carried out in groups. The collection values and encourages the use of previous knowledge and extra-curricular themes.

- Methodology in the use of didactic resources and extra activities

The development of skills such as generalizing and visualizing are highly stimulated. There are many challenges, problems with no solution or several solutions and opportunities for the student to formulate problems about the content developed and verify processes and results. Mental calculation, both arithmetic and algebraic, is highly valued. Calculators and drawing instruments are widely used as teaching resources.

Teacher's manual

- Theoretical foundation of the collection

In all volumes, the manual presents the theoretical foundation and guiding principles of the work, which are based on current knowledge in Mathematics Education.

- Guidelines for using the book

It also includes detailed instructions for using each book, comments, answers to questions and special activity sheets.

- Suggestions for extra activities, specific assessments and training

The assessment guidelines include suggestions for a variety of instruments, according to the content covered. It also offers suggestions for complementary activities and bibliography on various topics.

Mathematics: Ideas and Challenges - Iracema and Dulce

Content selection and distribution

- Covering the five fields of mathematics (numbers and operations, algebra and functions, geometry, quantities and measures, statistics and probability).

The collection focuses on the five fields of mathematics. It presents the content expected for this stage of schooling. However, a large number of activities focus on numerical and algebraic calculations, while other important topics, such as financial mathematics, receive little attention.

- Distribution and articulation of fields and contents

The fields of school mathematics alternate throughout the book and, in general, they are linked together. Concepts and procedures that have already been presented are almost always taken up again before others are introduced that expand on them. In the field of numbers and operations, there is an excess of calculation with radicals, while in the field of algebra, the emphasis is on presenting a large number of rules and procedures.

algebraic procedures, to the detriment of the use of symbolic language, in the field of geometry little attention is paid to spatial geometry.

To better visualize how the fields for each year in this collection are distributed, we have inserted a graph provided by the 2011 Textbook Guide.

Graph 2: Distribution of the fields in the collection Matematica- Ideias e Desafios

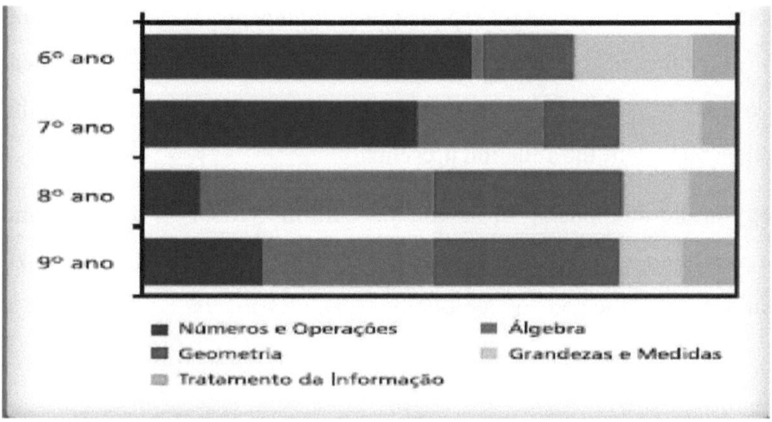

Source: Textbook Guide, 2011

Content approach

- Content approach in the field: Numbers and operations

The content is presented in the same way as in the 2008 PNLD, but in this PNLD rational numbers are not covered in the book for the 5th grade. [a]

- Content approach in the field: Algebra and functions

The contents are presented in the same way as the PNLD 2008.

- Approach to content in the field: Geometry

The contents are presented in the same way as the PNLD 2008.

- Approach to content in the field: Quantities and measures

The contents are presented in the same way as the PNLD 2008.

- Approach to content in the field: Statistics and probability

The contents are presented in the same way as the PNLD 2008.

Teaching-learning methodology

- Methodology in the student-context relationship

The units that make up the book begin with examples from a variety of contexts, with the aim of mobilizing students' interest and enabling the teacher to diagnose their previous knowledge. This is followed by explanations of concepts and procedures and some questions are proposed to encourage students to reflect on the mathematical content being worked on. However, in general, these questions do not encourage the exploration of other aspects of the situation presented.

- Methodology in the relationship of interaction with individuals (classmates and teacher) The *Exchange ideas and solve* sections, which are frequent, encourage the exchange of opinions, dialogue and cooperation between classmates.

- Methodology in the use of didactic resources and extra activities

The book emphasizes the use of some teaching resources, such as drawing and measuring instruments, as well as calculators.

Teacher's manual

- Theoretical foundation of the collection

In the collection, the theoretical foundations of the proposal are not clearly explained in the work's methodological choices.

- Guidelines for using the book

General didactic guidelines are given on the mathematical fields, which are accompanied by a table distributing the topics of these fields in the collection.

- Suggestions for extra activities, specific assessments and training.

The specific part of the supplement to the manual contains the content by unit, with objectives and indicators for assessment, as well as the solution to some activities. It also offers complementary texts and teaching guidelines. These, however, are very brief and do not constitute effective support material for teachers in the classroom. There are also suggestions for further reading and *websites* for continuing teacher training.

Comparative analysis of collections - PNLD 2011

The five fields of mathematics in the two collections continue to be presented throughout the grades. However, the collection *Matemàtica Ideias e Desafios - Iracema and Dulce,* continues to present an excess of calculation with radicals in the field of numbers and operations; in the field of algebra, the presentation of a large number of rules and algebraic procedures is privileged, to the detriment of the use of symbolic language; in the field of geometry, little attention is paid to spatial geometry, although articulation is made between the fields. In the *Mathematics - Imenes and Lellis* collection, the work continues to present significant links between different fields, in the texts and activities, as well as themes that have been taken up, deepened and expanded.

In the *Mathematics - Imenes and Lellis* collection, in terms of teaching and learning methodology, the student-context relationship continues with the discussion of the content through the *Talking about the text* section, the relationship of interaction with individuals is stimulated through the *Action* section and the methodology in the use of teaching resources and extra activities is encouraged, such as the use of calculators, drawing instruments and activities that encourage mental calculation. In the collection *Matemàtica Ideias e Desafios - Iracema e Dulce,* the methodology of interacting with individuals continues to stand out with special sections such as *Exchanging ideas and solving* with activities involving groups or the whole class, the use of drawing and measuring instruments.

As for the teacher's manual in the collection *Matemàtica - Imenes e Lellis,* it sets out the theoretical basis as well as the guiding principles of the work, and also provides detailed guidelines for the use of each book, guidelines on assessment and suggestions for complementary activities In the collection *Matemàtica Ideias e Desafios - Iracema e Dulce,* the manual briefly explains a supplement which contains the content by unit, with objectives and indicators for assessment, as well as the solution of some activities, complementary texts and teaching guidelines, but the theoretical foundations of the proposal are once again not clearly explained.

PNLD 2014

Mathematics - Imenes and Lellis

Content selection and distribution

- Covering the five fields of mathematics (numbers and operations, algebra and functions, geometry, quantities and measures, statistics and probability).

The five fields of mathematics appear throughout the collection. The study of numbers and operations gains significance both in its links with other fields of school mathematics and in the variety of tasks and strategies. The moderate use of rules reveals an effort to demystify the difficulties of learning algebra.

- Distribution and articulation of fields and contents

The fields are well distributed throughout each book and the collection as a whole. The central ideas are revisited several times, in the same volume and throughout the volumes, which is positive.

To better visualize how the fields for each year are distributed in this collection, we have inserted a graph provided by the 2014 Textbook Guide.

Graph 3: Distribution of the fields of Mathematics in the Matemàtica collection

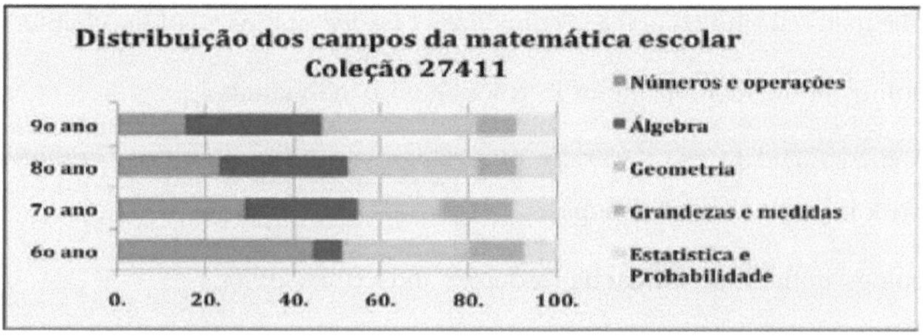

Source: Textbook Guide, 2014

Content approach

- Content approach in the field: Numbers and operations

The contents are presented in the same way as the PNLD 2011.

- Content approach in the field: Algebra and functions

The contents are presented in the same way as the PNLD 2011.

- Approach to content in the field: Geometry

The contents are presented in the same way as the PNLD 2011.

- Content approach in the field: Quantities and measures

The content is presented in the same way as in the PNLD 2011, but in this PNLD the content of proportionality between magnitudes is covered in the book for grade 7ª .

- Approach to content in the field: Statistics and probability

The content is presented in the same way as in the 2011 PNLD, but in this PNLD three chapters are devoted to the content of graphs, tables and arithmetic mean.

Teaching-learning methodology

- Methodology in the student-context relationship

The contents of the book are presented through theoretical explanations, followed by examples, some systematizations and activities. The *Talking* to learn section offers the opportunity to reflect on the content by asking the student to argue in writing or orally on a given topic. The systematization of the content is appropriate and there is also a summary of the material studied in the section *"Don't forget"* at the end of the chapters.

- Methodology in the relationship of interaction with individuals

Students are encouraged to use a variety of strategies to solve problems, compare results and work in pairs or small groups.

- Methodology in the use of didactic resources and extra activities

The concrete materials used in the book are simple, such as graph paper, tangrams, plannings, as well as molds for reproduction. Also noteworthy are the activities which call for the use of calculators and drawing and measuring instruments. Students are encouraged to work at home and are given tasks specifically for this purpose.

Teacher's manual

- Theoretical foundation of the collection

The book's guiding principles are: the stimulation of reasoning and argumentation in the construction of concepts, as well as a preference for socially relevant content.

- Guidelines for using the book

Há suggestions for planning lessons, with indications of what should be prioritized. There are also comments on the balance between the formal and the intuitive in the development of the content.

- Suggestions for extra activities, specific assessments and training

There are interesting suggestions for extra activities, which can be included in the teacher's planning. The guideline is for assessment to be global and based on different instruments. In addition, in each chapter, there are suggestions on how to assess the subject. There are sources for updating and improving teaching, including information from scientific societies, training and research centers, *websites,* publications, software and video programs.

Mathematics: Ideas and Challenges - Iracema and Dulce

Content selection and distribution

- Covering the five fields of mathematics (numbers and operations, algebra and functions, geometry, quantities and measures, statistics and probability).

The five fields of mathematics predominate in the collection. The contents selected make up an extensive and detailed list of mathematical topics that are usually intended for this stage of schooling, resulting in dense books with a high number of pages.

- Distribution and articulation of fields and contents.

The distribution of the fields of school mathematics in the volumes of the collection follows a pattern that is almost far from desirable: numbers and operations take up too much space in the 6th grade book; algebra predominates in the 7th grade; geometry and algebra take up almost all the attention in volumes 8 and 9; quantities and measures are concentrated only in the 6th grade. Despite this, the articulation between fields is a highlight of the collection, such as the use of statistical graphs in problems from other fields.

To better visualize how the fields for each year in this collection are distributed, we have inserted a graph provided by the 2014 Textbook Guide.

Graph 2: Distribution of the fields in the collection Matematica- Ideias e Desafios

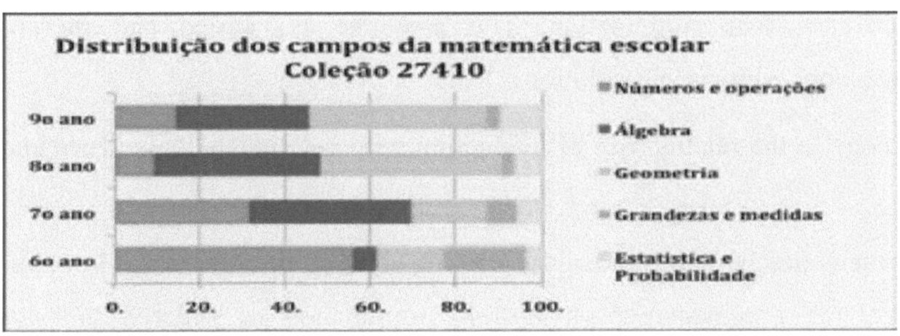

Source: Textbook Guide, 2014

Content approach

- Content approach in the field: Numbers and operations

The contents are presented in the same way as the PNLD 2011.

- Content approach in the field: Algebra and functions

The contents are presented in the same way as the PNLD 2011.

- Approach to content in the field: Geometry

The contents are presented in the same way as the PNLD 2011.

- Approach to content in the field: Quantities and measures

The content is presented in the same way as in the 2011 PNLD, but in this PNLD the content of numbers and measures is dealt with in the book for grade 5ª and in grades 7ª and 8ª the content of measures is brought in as part of the approach to the content of geometry and as part of the approach to the content of similarities.

- Approach to content in the field: Statistics and probability

The content is presented in the same way as in the PNLD 2011, but in the book for grade 6ª statistics is dealt with as part of the content of rational numbers and equations.

Teaching-learning methodology

- Methodology in the student-context relationship

In the collection, the content is often presented on the basis of interesting problem situations, but the solutions are presented immediately afterwards, which does not encourage active student participation. The activities are varied and present challenging questions with various solutions.

- Methodology in the relationship of interaction with individuals (colleagues and teacher)

Encouraging interaction between students is a strong point of the collection. However, situations involving argumentation, hypothesis formulation or generalization of concepts are rare. Although some justifications for procedures are presented, the early indication of "practical rules" does not guarantee that students will develop autonomous reasoning.

- Methodology in the use of didactic resources and extra activities

The situations in which concepts are revisited are often repetitive and lack depth. The calculator is used adequately, but the use of other technological resources is not suggested.

Teacher's manual

- Theoretical basis of the collection

The principles on which the collection is based and the methodology related to the various fields of school mathematics are adequately presented.

- Guidelines for using the book

The general structure of the collection and the objectives of each section are commented on, so as to guide the teacher in their use.

- Suggestions for extra activities, specific assessments and training.

There are few suggestions for complementary activities and only a few in-depth texts. Hά a text that discusses interesting suggestions for assessing students in Mathematics. There are suggestions for further reading, continuing education centers and *websites,* some of which are out of date.

Comparative analysis of collections - PNLD 2014

The five fields of mathematics in the two collections continue to be presented throughout the grades. However, the collection *Matemàtica Ideias e Desafios - Iracema and Dulce,* continues to present too much space in the field of numbers and operations in the 6th grade book; algebra predominates in the 7th grade; geometry and algebra take up almost all the attention in volumes 8 and 9; quantities and measures are concentrated only in the 6th grade, however the articulation between fields is a highlight in the collection. In the *Mathematics - Imenes and Lellis* collection, the fields continue to be well distributed throughout each book and the collection as a whole.

In the collection *Matemàtica- Imenes e Lellis,* in the teaching-learning methodology, the student-context relationship and the discussion of the content is carried out in the

Conversation section, the relationship of interaction with individuals is stimulated by working in pairs or small groups and the methodology of using didactic resources and extra activities is encouraged, such as the use of calculators, drawing instruments, graph paper, tangrams, plannings, as well as reproduction templates. In the collection Matemàtica *Ideias e Desafios - Iracema e Dulce*, the methodology of interacting with individuals is a strong incentive in the collection, the content is often presented on the basis of interesting problem situations and only the use of calculators is encouraged.

As for the teacher's manual in the collection *Matemàtica - Imenes e Lellis,* it contains suggestions for planning lessons, extra activities, assessment of the subject and sources for updating and improving teaching skills. In the collection *Matemàtica Ideias e Desafios - Iracema and Dulce,* the principles on which the collection is based are adequately presented, the general structure of the collection and the objectives of each section are commented on, there are few suggestions for supplementary activities, but more suggestions on assessing students in Mathematics and on continuing training centers.

FINAL CONSIDERATIONS

The aim of this work was to analyze the trajectory of two Mathematics collections that have been approved in the Textbook Guides for Primary School II in the last 15 years of triennial evaluation, knowing the importance that these guides play in the process of choosing textbooks. This will give us a closer look at the collections analyzed, raising possible discussions, especially in the process of choice by teachers.

Generally speaking, it is clear that the collections analyzed present approaches to mathematics that are relevant to the level at which they are aimed, which is why they are present in these evaluations. However, it is clear that there are some considerations from the point of view of the evaluators that differentiate them.

The various documents that govern the basic education curriculum, such as the PCN, emphasize the importance of innovative teaching, but for this to happen, a key factor is the auxiliary didactic tools used in teaching, such as textbooks, which must be in line with current teaching paradigms for the subjects who will use them. Of the collections analyzed, the one that comes closest to the characteristics focused on by the PCN is the collection *Matemàtica - Imenes e Lellis*, because in all the guides it was evaluated positively, always with good articulation between the fields, methodology presented in a clear and objective way, the teacher's manual was well-founded, with suggestions and guidance, whereas in the collection *Matemàtica Ideias e Desafios - Iracema and Dulce* there was almost always criticism of these points, such as the concentration of fields and the excessive emphasis on algebraic calculations. However, this collection has shown positive characteristics over the course of the evaluations, such as the presentation of contextualized problem situations, the appearance of orientations and guidelines in the teacher's manual, as well as the encouragement of games that stimulate interaction.

With a view to using the books to support learning issues in the classroom, the two collections encourage this through active and innovative methodologies with games and socialized activities.

As for the teachers' perspective, *there is* always a concern with continuing education, especially in the *Matemàtica- Imenes and Lellis* collection, indicating ways of improving and updating.

In the light of the above, we would stress that the Textbook Guides are an important resource for teachers to choose the ideal textbook to work with and for their students to study. In making this choice, the teacher must take into account the reality in which he or she is inserted, the social and cultural context that will directly interfere in the students' teaching and learning process. Our aim has not been to determine the most appropriate textbook to use, but to indicate the characteristics that each one possesses in order to make a plausible choice in relation to reality.

We emphasize that this work is of great relevance to elementary school math teachers, especially those in elementary school, as it provides support for choosing a textbook to use in math classes. Thus, the language used in the work has been succinct and objective so that there is no trace of doubt about the writing developed.

Therefore, in concluding this work, we believe it is important to develop other studies and research that contribute to and support the problem studied in choosing the textbook to be used in math classes, thus contributing to the students' teaching and learning process.

REFERENCES

BARRETO, B. de C; MONTEIRO, M. C. G. de G. **Professor, textbook and Contemporaneity**. Available at: http://www.maxwell.lambda.ele.puc-rio.br. Accessed on: 15/08/2012.

BOGDAN, R.; BIKLEN, S. **Qualitative research in education:** an introduction to theory and methods. Porto: Porto Editora, 1994.

BORATO, D. L *et al.* **The textbook as an instrument for the construction of subjectivity in the process of consolidating the school curriculum**. 2004. Available at: www.olhoscriticos.com.br/site1/arquivos-online/texto-o-livro-didatico.pdf.

Accessed on July 3, 2015.

BARDIN, L. **Content Analysis** (Translated by Luis Antero Reto and Augusto Pinheiro). Sao Paulo: Ediçôes 70, 2011.

BRASIL. **PNLD 2008 Textbook Guide:** Mathematics. Brasilia: MEC, 2007 .
National Curriculum Parameters: Introduction. Secretaria de Educaçao Fundamental, Brasilia: MEC/SEF, 1997.

. **Guide to textbooks:** PNLD 2012: Presentation. - Brasilia: Ministry

da Educaçao, Secretaria de Educaçao Bàsica, 2011a.

National Textbook Program. Ministry of Education.

Available at: <http://www.mec.gov.br> Accessed on: 30 Nov. 2014.

CARDOSO, E. R.; BENEVIDES-PEREIRA, A. M. T. **Affective influences in the teaching and learning of Mathematics.** In: IX Congresso Nacional de Educaçao - EDUCACERE, Oct. 26-29; Curitiba: Champagnat. 2009, p. 3024-3035.

CARVALHO, P. C. P. **Doing Mathematics and using Mathematics.** Leap into the future. Series Matemàtica não é problema. Available at

<http://www.tvebrasil.com.br/SALTO/boletins2005/boletins2005.htm>.

D'AMBROSIO, U. **Da realidade à açâo: reflexôes sobre educaçâo e matemàtica. -**

Sao Paulo: Summus; Campinas: Ed. da Universidade Estadual de Campinas, 1986.

FERREIRA, A. B. de H. **Mini Aurélio - Dicionârio. 4th Edition**, Nova Fronteira, 2001.

FRANCISCO FILHO, G. **História Geral da Educaçâo.** Campinas: Alinea, 2005.

GOMES, Daiane. **The textbook in the process of teaching and learning mathematics: Considerations of public school teachers in Ji-Paranâ.**

2014. 49f. Monograph (Degree in Mathematics) - Department of Mathematics and Statistics, Federal University of Rondônia, Ji-Paranà.

LAJOLO, M. (org). **Textbooks: an (almost) user manual.** In: Em aberto. INEP. v.16. n° 69, 1996.

MANTOVANI, K. P. **The National Textbook Program - PNLD: Impacts on the Quality of Public Education**. 2009. Dissertation (Master's Degree in Human Geography) - Faculty of Philosophy, Letters and Human Sciences, University of Sao Paulo. 2009.

MIRANDA, S. R; LUCA, T. R. **O livro didâtico de história de hoje: um panorama a partir do PNLD.** In: Revista Brasileira de História, v. 24, n° 48. Sao Paulo: 2004.

NASCIMENTO, L. F. **History and nature of science: a roadmap for textbook analysis**. Master's dissertation. Campina Grande: UEPB, 2011.

OLIVEIRA, J. B. A. e; GUIMARÂES, S. D. P; BOMÉNY, H. M. B. **A politica do livro didâtico**. Sao Paulo: Summus; Campinas: Editora da Universidade Estadual de Campinas, 1984.

PERNAMBUCO, S. de E. **Base Curricular Comum para as Redes Pùblicas de Ensino de Pernambuco: matemàtica** / Secretaria de Educaçao. - Recife: SE. 2008.

PONTE, J. P. **The teaching of Mathematics in Portugal: Lessons from the past, challenges for the future.** 2004.

ROMANATTO, M. C. **The textbook: scope and limits.** In: VII ENCONTRO PAULISTA DE EDUCAÇÂO MATEMÀTICA, 2004, Sao Paulo. Proceedings. Sao

Paulo, 2004.

SANTOS, F. M. dos. **Content analysis: Laurence Bardin's vision.** Revista Eletrônica de Educaçao. 2012. Available at: <http://www.reveduc.ufscar.br>. Accessed on: 08 Aug. 2015.

SILVEIRA, M. R. A. **"Matemàtica é dificil": A preconstituted meaning evidenced in students' speech**, 2002. Available at:

<http://www.anped.org.br/25/marisarosaniabreusilveirat19.rtf>.

SPOSILO, E. S. **Textbooks in geography, from the evaluation process to their choice.** In: PAVÂO, Antonio Carlos. The textbook in question. Program: Salto para o Futuro/TV Escola. 2006. p. 23-37.

MIX
Papier aus verantwortungsvollen Quellen
Paper from responsible sources
FSC® C105338

Printed by Books on Demand GmbH, Norderstedt / Germany